CW00411047

dEcoRatiNG CERAMICS

Written by Kelly Smith
Illustrated by Carol Daniel

With kind thanks to the artists and staff of All Fired Up, Ipswich, Suffolk

TOP THAT!™

Copyright © 2005 Top That! Publishing Inc,
25031 W. Avenue Stanford, Suite #60,
Valencia, CA 91355
www.topthatpublishing.com

CONTENTS

INTRODUCTION

Decorating ceramics is fast becoming an activity enjoyed by many people who are keen to explore their creativity. Painting on ceramics is fun and relaxing for all ages, and the finished items have many practical and decorative uses.

With the increasing availability of plain ceramics, the wide selection of paints in craft stores, and the growing popularity of ceramics cafés in the malls or on main street, homes are becoming filled with plates, mugs, and bowls decorated by their owners for use on a daily basis. Equally, gifts can be created with love and pride, and great memories can be captured, to be treasured for many years.

In this book, you will be introduced to a number of simple techniques for decorating ceramics that are easy to follow. The pieces in this book have been decorated by different artists to show the versatility of this craft. Everyone can decorate ceramics, regardless of artistic ability, and even the simplest of designs can look stunning.

The projects in this book cover most of the common techniques for decorating ceramics, and use paints that can either be set in your oven at home (like those provided in the kit), or paints which are fired in a kiln. You can use whichever paint you prefer; just adapt the design to suit the paint's consistency.

Whether you start with an easy project or something more advanced from the selection included here, simply follow the step-by-step guidelines and surprise yourself by creating something truly special!

MATERIALS & equipment

CERAMICS

In this book, you will be working with two types of ceramics—unglazed and glazed.

Unglazed ceramics are more commonly found in craft stores and ceramics cafés and are often referred to as bisque ware. The surface is slightly rough and dry to the touch. These ceramics have been fired once, and will need to be glazed and fired in a kiln either before or after painting.

Glazed ceramics have already been coated with glaze and fired in a kiln. These ceramics are shiny. You can purchase these in department stores and china stores. Some stores specialize in selling plain, white ceramics which will give you plenty of choice.

GLAZED CERAMIC PAINTS

The paints provided with this book are suitable for applying on a glazed surfac such as glass, porcelain, tiles, and ceramics. This paint can be used to decorate objects for use in rooms where moisture is high, such as bathrooms or kitchens. To set the colors, place in the oven, at a temperature of 150°C/ 300 °F/gas mark 2 for fifteen minutes.

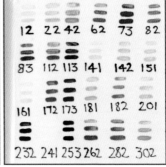

Although these paints are waterproof when set, you should not serve food on the finished dis as the paint can chip. To clean your painted object, use a sponge and soapy water. Acrylic paints and othe porcelain and ceramic paints can be use on glazed ceramics, follow the manufacture instructions for the best results.

UNDER-GLAZE PAINTS

As the name suggests, under-glaze colors are used on unglazed ceramics, or bisque, that are then glazed and fired in a kiln at a very high temperature. They are water-based and non-toxic. Therefore any mistakes made during painting can be removed with clean water, and clothes do not need treating prior to washing if splashed with under-glaze paint.

Once glazed, the ceramic is completely safe for use with food and drink. It should be washed with warm, soapy water—but you should avoid putting any of your painted ceramics in a dishwasher.

Naturally, most people won't have a kiln at home but you'll find that many ceramics cafés and stores will offer a firing service. Make some phone calls to find the right price for you.

BRUSHES

Ceramics paints are normally applied with a brush, the size of which will depend on your design. It is best to have a selection handy. You may also find an outliner brush or "pen" useful.

PALETTE

You will need a palette for your paint. Paper plates are very useful as they can be thrown away when you are finished, but you could equally use an old dish or ice cream lid. Artists' palettes can also be used but initially they're an unnecessary expense.

STAMPS AND STENCILS

Many craft stores sell rubber and foam stamps and stencils, which can be used for decorating walls, greeting cards or painting on ceramics. In recent years, the internet has become a great place to find stamp and stencil companies selling a wide selection of designs. Alternatively, you can make your own by using uncut stencil material, or thick sheets of acetate. Simply draw your design directly onto the sheet, or use a photocopied design, and cut it out using a craft knife.

Spray adhesive is ideal for positioning your stencil on your ceramic. A stamp roller and a sponge are useful tools to purchase as well.

MASKING

A number of materials can be used to "mask" a ceramic, allowing you to apply paint over the top.

Masking tape and sticky tape can be used when you need a straight line.

Stickers found in craft stores and stationery stores can allow you to create interesting designs, as can shapes cut out of paper when held or temporarily stuck onto the ceramic.

Alternatively, you can purchase masking fluid from art stores, which can be applied onto the ceramic and peeled off once you have painted over it.

TRACING

Tracing paper or thin "printer" paper and a regular #2 pencil are very useful tools to assist you in decorating your ceramics. It is also helpful to keep an eraser, pencil sharpener, and ruler close at hand to assist in your planning of a project (see page 10 for instructions).

SGRAFFITO TOOL

A sgraffito tool is used to create a design by scraping paint away, leaving a white line. These tools can be purchased from a craft store. Alternatively, you can carefully use a sharp instrument such as a pair of compasses.

SPONGES

Applying paint with different sponges can produce unusual and interesting effects on ceramics. A natural sponge has random holes which are often further apart, while a synthetic sponge has holes which are closer together and more uniform. The amount of paint on the sponge will also affect the results so experiment on old tiles first.

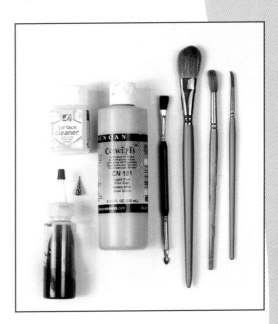

BASIC techniques

PAINTING

Begin by preparing your ceramic according to the directions provided by the manufacturer. You may need to apply a surface cleaner, an undercoat, alcohol, or soapy water prior to painting. The paints supplied need to be applied to a clean, grease-free, and dry glazed ceramic (often being left overnight to dry completely). When ready to paint, make sure you have all your tools to hand, including some clean water and a sponge—useful for correcting mistakes.

Be prepared to try things out and explore different effects. Different brushes produce different results—from broad swathes of color with a thick brush, to painting over signatures with a fine brush. Keep experimenting and don't expect perfection first time—old tiles will come in handy for your early attempts when using acrylic-based paints.

As you paint more you will become accustomed to using the paints, their consistency, and appearance when dr Under-glaze colors change dramatically in appearance after glazing and the more coats of under-glaze you apply, th stronger the color after firing.

When applying your paints, always use the light colors as your background colors. Darker colors should be used later for details and decorations. Avoid painting light shades on top of dark colors, as they do not show up well and the results can be disappointing.

DOT WORK

Dots can be used to produce a variety of designs—as can be seen from the examples in this book. Before you begin to paint dots onto your ceramic, it is a good idea to plan your design, either on a piece of paper or directly on your item using a pencil. The paint can then be applied in dots using a short-haired brush.

A different dot method is to use a toothbrush to splash the paint onto your ceramic. By dipping the toothbrush into the paint, then using your finger to bend the bristles back, you will produce a fine mist effect which looks especially attractive when a number of different colors are used. This technique has been used on the cruet set project on page 24.

SPONGING

It's fun to experiment with the variety of finishes you can achieve with the use of both natural and synthetic sponges. Many designs can be inspired by the paint effects produced by using them. Sponges are also very useful when using other techniques such as masking, stamping, and stenciling.

When using a sponge, pour your paint onto a palette and dip the edge of your sponge in. It is better to apply a small amount of paint and add to it to build the depth of the colors. Once again, begin by sponging the lighter colors, then apply the darker shades later. Sponging onto wet paint will create a different effect as the colors merge, or you may prefer to leave each color to dry between applications.

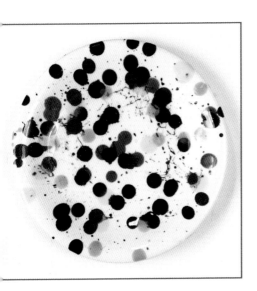

STENCILING

Stencils are easy to use, but you may need some masking tape or spray adhesive to hold your stencil in place. You can then apply the paint directly over the stencil with either a flat-cut bristle stencil brush, or a sponge. Don't worry if the paint smudges under the stencil, as you can always use some water to clean the excess paint away.

STAMPING

When using stamps to decorate ceramics, a stamp roller or sponge are ideal for applying the paint to the stamp. Using a brush often results in too much paint being applied to the stamp, which produces a rather blotchy picture when you press the stamp onto the ceramic.

It is a good idea to experiment on some paper before you stamp on the ceramic as this will help you decide how much paint you need to get the finish you are looking for.

TRACING

Tracing is an excellent way of transferring a design or writing onto ceramics. Simply draw the design onto tracing paper or thin white paper, turn the paper over and use your pencil to draw over the back of the design. With the design right-side up, place it on your ceramic and draw over your design a third time. The graphite on the back of the paper will then be transferred lightly onto the ceramic.

One important rule to remember: any pencil work on unglazed ceramics disappears completely during the firing process. Therefore, if you want to see it, you have to paint it!

MASKING

If your design requires a dark background and a light or white area, then masking is an ideal technique. Stickers and masking tape are applied and you then paint the background color directly onto the ceramic, using as many coats as necessary to achieve the desired depth of color. When the paint is dry, you simply peel the sticker or tape away, revealing the white ceramic underneath. You can then either leave this, or apply a different color.

Masking fluid follows the same principle except that as a liquid it needs to be applied with a brush. It will set quickly, however, so wash your brush immediately after use with very hot water to avoid clogging the bristles. Once the fluid is set, you can paint over it and peel the mask away once your paint is dry.

SGRAFFITO

Sgraffito is a very simple technique which can create impressive results. Begin by painting a solid background on your ceramic, or an area of —apply a number of coats if you want the color to be very dense. Once the paint is dry, you then use your sgraffito tool or pair of compasses to scrape the paint off the ceramic. The white lines create your design.

MIXING colors

Mixing your own colors isn't difficult, but don't expect the fired results to look the same as your liquid paint. Basic color theories and principles apply but you'll still get a different shade each time—that just makes life more interesting!

COLOR wheel

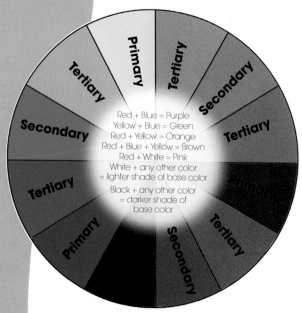

Primary

Tertiary

Secondary

Tertiary

Secondary

Tertiary

Primary

Primary

Tertiary

Secondary

Red + Blue = Purple
Yellow + Blue = Green
Red + Yellow = Orange
Red + Blue + Yellow = Brown
Red + White = Pink
White + any other color
= lighter shade of base color
Black + any other color
= darker shade of
base color

Experiment with smaller or larger amounts of each to obtain different shades and strengths of color.
The color wheel opposite allows you to see the different shades available from the three primary colors.

READY-MIXED COLORS

You will find as you mix your paints that some colors are more easily achieved than others. Certain colors will appear slightly "muddy," and it is easier to buy the exact shade you require to avoid this. Remember also that it is difficult to mix exactly the same shade twice; if you plan to paint an item over several days, or have large areas to fill with the same color, mixing your own paint could cause problems. A ready-mixed color will allow you to stop and start at your leisure without the worry of re-mixing the color to match.

PAINT PALETTE

The basic color rules of paints also apply to ceramic paints: mix blue and yellow to create green, blue and red to create purple, and red and yellow to create orange.

DAISY daisy

ARTIST: Michele Dean

colors

This delightful flower mug has been created using a very simple version of the dot technique. You can use the same colors shown here or experiment with different shades.

You will need:

A glazed mug
A pencil and paper
A marker pen
Red, white, blue, green, yellow, and
  purple ceramic paints
A palette
A fine brush
Water, for washing your brush
Sponge
Spray varnish (optional)

Daisy Template

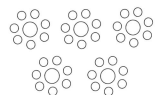

1) Clean your mug with soapy water to remove any dirt or grease, and leave to dry overnight.

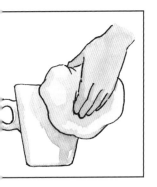

2) Plan your design by sketching the mug on paper first, planning the flower colors to ensure that no two flowers of the same color are next to each other. Using your marker pen, mark the center dot for each flower directly on the mug, making sure you allow enough space for each flower and its petals.

3 Shake your pots of paint well before beginning to paint. Pour the paints onto your palette or paper plate. Dip the tip of the brush into the white paint and dot the paint on to the center of each flower.

4 Wash your brush thoroughly and dab dry on the sponge (or you could use paper towels). Choose a different color, dip your brush in the paint, and dot the paint around the center white dot six times, to create the petal effect. Repeat this step with all the colors to complete your flower mug.

5 Allow the paint to dry then bake in the oven at 150°C/300°F/gas mark 2 for fifteen minutes (or follow the manufacturer's instructions if different), or apply a spray varnish.

HANDY HINT: *Remember; keep your mug for decoration only if painting onto glazed ceramics. This design works just as well with underglaze or acrylic paints.*

BLUE moods

ARTIST: Maureen Galvani

colors

Creating your own tiles using stamps is a simple and effective way to personalize your home. Choose colors and themes that complement your rooms, and experiment with a combination of techniques to create your unique design. The tiles can then be used on the walls, as coasters or pot stands.

You will need:

Bisque tile(s)
Water, for washing your tools
A cloth
A pencil and paper
Flower stamp
Blue under-glaze paint
A palette
A medium brush
A stamp roller or sponge
A craft knife
Glaze

1. Wash your bisque tile or tiles with clean water. Dry thoroughly with a lint-free cloth.

2. Plan your designs by sketching them on paper first. It is a good idea to practice using the stamp on paper before you start working on the actual tiles. This allows you to assess how much paint you need to apply in order to get the desired effect.

3. Shake the paints well before pouring them onto your palette or plate. For the background of the tile create a wash by watering down the blue paint. Then, using the brush, apply loose, broad strokes across the tile, keeping all marks in the same direction. Leave this layer of paint to dry.

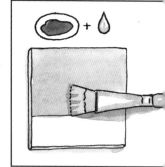

) Using the stamp roller or a sponge, apply paint to your stamp and press the stamp firmly onto the tile. Ensure you have applied even pressure to the surface of the stamp before lifting it carefully to reveal the picture on the tile. Repeat

this process until you have a few flowers on the tile, some of them going off the edge for a more interesting effect.

) Once dry, use a craft knife to scrape away part of the petals leaving only an outline. Do this with two of the flowers.

) Apply two coats of brush-on glaze and leave the tile to dry overnight again. The tile can then be placed in a kiln and fired at a temperature recommended by the glaze manufacturer.

TREE of life

ARTIST: Melanie Randall

colors

You will need:

A glazed vase
A stencil
Spray adhesive (optional)
Masking tape
Red, white, blue, green, and yellow
   ceramic paints
A palette
Paper towels
A stencil brush
Water, for washing your tools
A sponge
Spray varnish (optional)

The Tree of Life is a traditional Shaker
symbol, dating back hundreds of years.
This beautiful vase has been created using
a stencil and some masking tape, and is a
perfect example of how a simple design
can be extremely
appealing.

Clean your
   vase to remove
any dirt or grease
and leave to
dry overnight.

2. Apply the stencil (see handy hint
over the page) to the vase with
masking tape or spray adhesive. Apply
two parallel strips of masking tape
around the base of the vase to create a
narrow line.

3. Shake your pots of paint well before
beginning to paint. Pour the paints
onto your palette or paper plate. Dip
your stencil brush into the paint and
dab off any excess paint on a paper
towel. Keeping the brush at right angles
to the vase use a dabbing action to
apply the
green paint to
the leaves.
Allow to dry for
one hour.

(4) Using the same action, apply the red and yellow paint to the apples and leave to dry for another hour (leaving the paint to dry each time will limit accidental smudges).

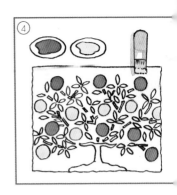

(5) Mix yellow, blue, and red paint together to make a brown and use this paint for the trunk and the boughs.

(6) When the paint is dry, use a small sponge (or carefully use the stencil brush) to lightly dab green paint to the edge of the apples to create a softer look. Dab green paint between the masking tape strips at the bottom of the vase.

(7) When all the paint is completely dry, remove the masking tape and stencil cleanly and carefully.

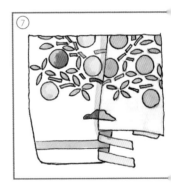

(8) Allow the paint to dry completely then bake in the oven at 150°C/ 300°F/gas mark 2 for fifteen minutes (or follow the manufacturer's instructions if different), or apply a spray varnish.

HANDY HINT: Making a Stencil

If you aren't able to find a similar tree stencil in your local craft store then you can easily make your own. Take a thick sheet of acetate, or see-through plastic, and trace the template on p 56. Block the areas to be cut out in black then carefully cut out these sections using a craft knife. If you want a bigger design you could simply enlarge the template using a photocopier.

PAINT a pitcher

ARTIST: Melanie Randall

colors

You will need:

A glazed jug
Red, white, blue, green, yellow, and
    purple ceramic paints
A palette
A sponge
Water, for washing your tools
A sgrafitto tool or similar
A fine brush
Spray varnish (optional)

*The abstract design on this attractive jug
(pictured on page 23) has been
created using a sponge, paint brush,
and a sgrafitto tool. Follow the easy steps
below to create your own colorful
masterpiece.*

1   Clean your jug with soapy water
    and leave to dry.

2   Shake your pots of paint well before
    beginning to paint. Pour your paint
onto your palette or paper plate. Dip
your sponge into the yellow paint and
sponge five circular splodges around the
belly of the jug. Wash your sponge well
and squeeze out any excess water.

Now sponge four slightly smaller
green splodges above and below
the line of the yellow splodges and
in the gap between.

3   Using the purple paint, sponge five
    smaller splodges around the neck
of the jug. Be careful to apply the paint
gently and sparingly. Working quickly,
while the paint is still wet, scratch a spiral
design through
the paint with
a sgrafitto tool
or a cocktail
stick. Allow the
paint to dry for
one hour.

4 Having allowed the yellow paint to dry, apply red paint with your sponge as before, concentrating the sponging in the center of the yellow splodge. Lighten the dabbing action as you radiate from the middle outward to allow the yellow underneath to show through.

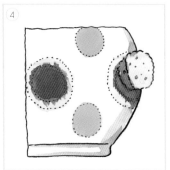

5 Repeat this process, using blue paint over the green splodges, but make sure the green paint is dry first or you'll end up blending the colors together.

6 When the two-tone colored splodges are dry, paint the spiral design over the top using a fine brush and white paint.

7 Invert the jug. Sponge purple paint gently around the base of the jug. Working quickly as before, scratch dots though the paint to reveal the body color underneath.

8 Allow the paint to dry completely then bake in the oven at 150°C/300°F/gas mark 2 for fifteen minutes (or follow the manufacturer's instructions if different) or apply a spray varnish. Now stand back and admire your work!

HANDY HINT:

Instead of using one sponge have a selection of sponges, one for each color, and use smaller sponges for the smaller splodges—you'll find it easier to to reduce the concentration of the second color as you radiate outward.

SALLY & percy

ARTIST: Hannah Berridge

colors

These stylish salt and pepper pots will add a personal touch to your dining table and can be created in colors to match your décor. This project is quick and simple, using the wash and splashing techniques, ideal when you're in the mood to be messy!

1. Wash your cruet set with clean water—alcohol-based cleaners should be avoided in case they taint the insides.

2. Take your large brush, moisten with water, and then dip it in the blue paint—the brush needs to be quite heavily loaded with liquid. Paint a large random brush stroke on each pot. Repeat this a few times, leaving areas of the pots white. Allow the paint to dry.

3. Clean your brush in water. Repeat the painting by dipping your brush in teal-colored paint and brushing it over the pots, layering the colors in places. Again, leave the paint to dry.

You will need:

Bisque salt and pepper pots
Fine and thick brushes
Water, for washing your tools
Under-glaze paints including
    dark blue, light blue, and teal
A toothbrush
A palette
Glaze
Paper towels (optional)

4. Now dip your toothbrush in the dark blue paint, pull the bristles back with your finger, then release them slowly so the paint splatters over the pots. Leave to dry.

5. Using the medium brush, paint the words "salt" and "pepper" with dark blue paint. Allow to dry and apply two further coats of the dark blue paint over the lettering.

6. Apply two coats of brush-on glaze and leave the salt and pepper pots to dry overnight. They can then be placed in a kiln and fired at a temperature recommended by the glaze manufacturer.

SAFE savings

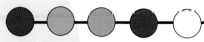

colors

ARTIST: Maureen Galvani

Imagine the pleasure on a child's face when they receive this fabulous piggy bank! Saving their allowance will suddenly seem a much more attractive proposition!

You will need:

A bisque piggy bank
A lint-free cloth
A pencil
Masking tape (optional)
Under-glaze paints, including red,
    blue, turquoise, and mustard yellow
A palette
Fine and medium brushes
Water, for washing your tools
A sgrafitto tool
Glaze

1. Wash your bisque piggy bank with clean water. Dry thoroughly with a lint-free cloth.

2. Using a pencil, draw straight lines on the surface of the piggy bank to create the block pattern. You may find it easier to use masking tape to provide the lines. Lightly pencil the initial of your chosen color on each square—it's easy to get lost while you're painting and put two identical colors next to each other.

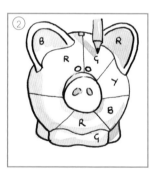

3. Pour the paints onto your palette. Using a medium brush, paint the squares, one color at a time. For a bold finish, you should apply three coats of paint to each block. Under-glaze paint dries very quickly but make sure each coat is dry before you add the next.

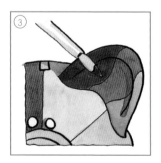

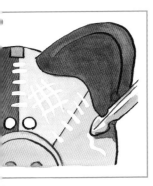

Once all the paint is dry use the sgrafitto tool to scratch the paint away to reveal the white bisque below. A variety of designs such as stars, squiggles, hatches, and swirls can add interest to your finished piggy bank. Scrape detail into the center of the squares first, then scratch half-inch long lines joining the colors to appear as stitches, creating a patchwork effect.

5) Using a fine brush and black paint, add two eyes.

Apply two coats of brush-on glaze and leave the piggy bank to dry overnight again. The piggy bank can then be placed in a kiln and fired at a temperature recommended by the glaze manufacturer.

FELINE fish supper

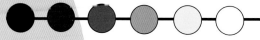

colors

ARTIST: Dasha Belotsvetova

You will need:

A glazed pet bowl
A pencil and paper
A fine marker pen
Orange, brown, black, yellow, red, and
   white ceramic paints
Fine and medium brushes
A palette
Water, for washing your tools
Spray varnish (optional)

*Your cat will have no doubt whose bowl
this is! This fun project is easily achieved
with a marker pen and some paint, and
before you know it, Felix won't be able to
stay away from the prospect of fish
bones for supper!*

(1) Clean your pet bowl with soapy
water to remove any dirt or grease,
and leave to dry.

(2) Plan your bowl by sketching the
design on paper first, referring to
the template on page 57 if you want to
replicate the example shown. Now use
the marker pen to draw the design onto
the bowl, taking care not to smudge the
lines as you draw.

(3) Shake your pots of paint well
before beginning to paint. Using a
fine paintbrush, outline your design,
along the side of the bowl and inside, in
black paint. Allow the paint to dry for
one hour.

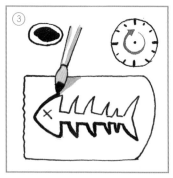

4) Using a medium brush, fill in the orange of the cat's face, leaving the features, nose, and inside of the ears unpainted for now.

5) Wash the medium brush out before applying the brown to the inside of paws—be careful not to go over the black outline.

6) Mix some of the black paint with the white paint to make a gray. Using the medium brush again, fill in the four fish skeletons along the sides. Leave all the paint to dry.

7) Use the fine brush to add the details such as the whiskers and eyes on the cat, and fish eyes. Wash your brush out thoroughly as you change color.

8) On the inside of the bowl, use the yellow paint and a medium brush to follow the black outline of the cat's face and paw prints. The yellow may overlap here but don't worry: happy accidents like these just add to the charm of hand painted ceramics.

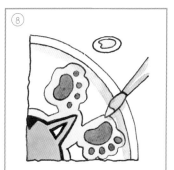

29

9. Use the fine brush to paint the middle of the cat's nose red, and add pink to the inside of the ears.

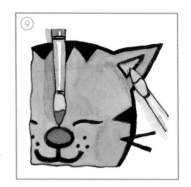

10. On the front side of the bowl use red, yellow, and orange paint to follow the black outline of "felix"— naturally you should change this to your pet's name. The small brown paw is similarly outlined in orange paint.

11. Allow all the paint to dry completely. The length of time can vary so read the manufacturer's instructions carefully but allow for at least three days.

12. Bake in the oven at 150°C/300°F/ gas mark 2 for fifteen minutes (or follow the manufacturer's instructions if different), or apply a spray varnish.

HANDY HINT:

If painting the outline with a fine brush is a little too tricky, tubes of ceramic and porcelain outliner are available. These are fitted with small nozzles that can be easier to master as the paint is often quite thick. Also available in some craft stores are ceramic marker pens; results and depth of color won't always match your paints, but they are certainly worth a try if you want precision.

NURSERY rhymes

ARTIST: Melanie Randall

colors

You will need:

A glazed egg cup
Green, yellow, black, and white
    ceramic paints
A fine marker pen
A palette
Water, for washing your brush
A fine brush
Spray varnish (optional)

1) Clean your egg cup with soapy
    water to remove any dirt or grease.
hake your pots of paint well before
eginning to paint.

2) Draw your design on the egg cup
    using the fine marker pen; two
heep, one opposite the other. Any lines
ou don't paint over can be rubbed
way with a damp sponge.

3) Cut your sponge into small pieces.
    Pour your paint onto your palette
r paper plate. Lightly dab green
round the base of the egg cup to
reate the grass.

HANDY HINT:

*If you don't want to draw the design
directly onto the egg cup use the
tracing paper method discussed on
page 10 to transfer your design. A
template can be found on page 57.*

4. Mix black and white paint to make a light gray and sponge this paint to form the two bodies of the sheep. Allow the paint to dry.

5. Mix some black and white paint to make a darker gray then gently sponge the dark gray paint over some of the light gray paint to create the impression of texture for the sheep's bodies. Allow the paint to dry.

6. Using a fine brush, paint the sheep's heads and legs, and the writing around the top of the egg cup with black paint.

7. Wash your brush thoroughly and now paint the yellow flowers. Clean your brush again and use white paint for the eyes and add a final dot of black once this layer has dried.

8. Bake in the oven at 150°C/300°F/ gas mark 2 for fifteen minutes (or follow the manufacturer's instructions if different), or apply a spray varnish.

HANDY HINT:

As with the jug project featured earlier, you may find it easier to work on one side of the egg cup at a time, resting the cup on an old cloth or using some sticky putty to keep it steady.

CITRUS flavors

ARTIST: Hannah Berridge

colors

You will need:

A bisque fruit bowl
A pencil
Masking fluid
A palette
A fine, medium, and thick brush
Boiling water with washing-up liquid
Under-glaze paints including blue,
    orange, yellow, and green
A pair of compasses (optional)
Glaze

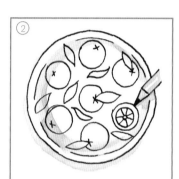

ruit will look delicious in this brightly-
olored fruit bowl. The technique of
nasking has been used to create the
vid contrast of colors, allowing you to
pply your paint liberally.

Wash your bisque fruit bowl with
clean water. Allow the bowl to dry.

Using a pencil, draw the design of
the oranges and leaves directly onto
ur bowl. Use the template on page 58
you don't want to draw it freehand. You
an use an eraser to correct any
nistakes as you draw.

3) Pour some masking fluid onto your
    palette and, using a fine brush,
paint the masking fluid onto the oranges
and leaves. Wash your brush in boiling
water with washing-up liquid
immediately after use to avoid the
masking fluid setting on your brush.

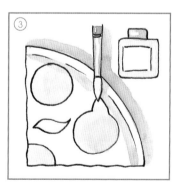

4 Once the masking fluid on the bowl is dry, use your thick brush to paint a coat of blue paint all over the bowl. You can paint directly over the masking fluid. Leave the paint to dry then apply more coats in the same way, until you are happy with the depth of color.

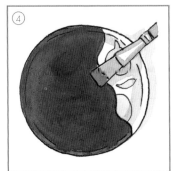

5 Once the blue paint is completely dry, gently peel the masking fluid away. A safety pin or pair of compasses can be very useful to help start the peeling process.

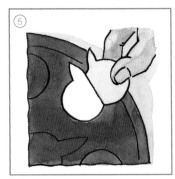

6 Pour some orange and green paint onto your palette, take your medium brush, and paint the oranges and then the leaves, washing the brush between colors, and leaving a white border.

7 Apply at least two coats, leaving the paint to dry between coats, preferably overnight.

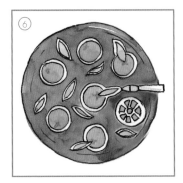

8 Apply two coats of brush-on glaze and leave the bowl to dry overnight again. The fruit bowl can then be placed in a kiln and fired at a temperature recommended by the glaze manufacturer.

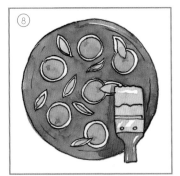

TIME for tea

ARTIST: Dasha Belotsvetova

colors

You will need:

Cleaning fluid
A glazed teapot
Purple, black, and green ceramic paints
A pencil and paper
Card
A craft knife
A cutting mat
Masking tape
Spray adhesive (optional)
A marker pen
A sponge
A palette
A fine brush
Spray varnish (optional)
Water, for washing your tools

Taking inspiration from the well-known designer Charles Rennie Mackintosh, this teapot has been stylishly decorated using a stencil created by the artist.

(1) Clean your teapot with soapy water to remove any dirt or grease and allow to dry. Shake your pots of paint well before beginning to paint.

(2) Plan your design by sketching the motifs on paper first. Alternatively, you could use the templates on pages 58-59. When you are happy with your design, re-draw the motifs for the sides and lid of the teapot onto pieces of card.

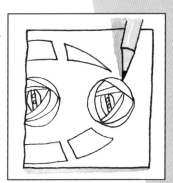

(3) Using a craft knife and a cutting mat, remove the inside areas of the designs to create three stencils.

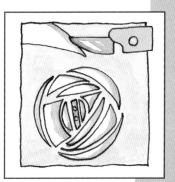

4 Use masking tape or spray adhesive, attach each stencil in turn to the side of the teapot, completing each section before moving onto the next.

5 Take your marker pen and draw around the inside edge of the first stencil to transfer the design onto the teapot. Remove the stencil. Any mistakes can be rubbed away with a damp sponge.

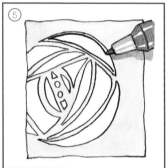

6 Use the same technique to transfer your designs onto the lid and opposite side.

7 Shake the paints and pour them onto your palette. Using your fine brush, paint the guidelines made with the marker pen. Allow the paint to dry for one hour.

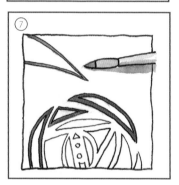

8 Use the medium brush to fill in blocks of color following the guidelines. Repeat on the other sections of the teapot.

9 Allow the paint to dry completely. Bake in the oven at 150°C/300°F/ gas mark 2 for fifteen minutes (or follow the manufacturer's instructions if different), or apply a spray varnish.

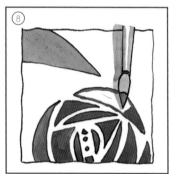

40

SPOT to dot

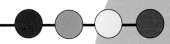

colors

You will need:

A glazed serving platter
A pencil and paper
A marker pen
Orange, brown, red, and yellow
    ceramics paints
A palette or paper plate for your paint
A fine brush
Water, for washing your tools
Spray varnish (optional)

This amazing serving platter has been created with hundreds of dots, in an Aboriginal design. Although simple to create, the results are truly impressive and worthy of display in a very prominent place.

① Wash your serving platter with soapy water and leave to dry overnight.

② Plan your designs by sketching on paper first. Use the fine marker pen to draw the design onto your platter. Alternatively you can use the template on page 60.

HANDY HINT:

Why not mount your platter on the wall in place of a picture? It's sure to be a talking point!

3 Shake your pots of paint well before beginning to paint. Pour your paint onto your palette or paper plate. Use your fine brush to paint over the design, beginning with the continuous lines.

4 With the tip of your brush, begin to apply small dots of color to fill in the outline areas of your design. Start with the yellow paint working on the central flower first. Leave for an hour before changing colors.

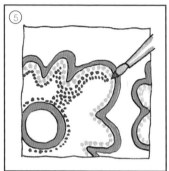

5 Using a clean brush, apply dots of red paint to the platter, but not the lip of the bowl in case you smudge it— it's best to paint this section of red last.

6 After another hour you can paint in all of the brown dots. Throughout your painting don't skimp on the color; an Aboriginal style design such as this needs clean, crisp dots in strong colors.

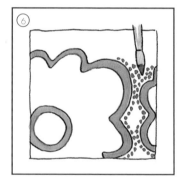

7 Finish the painting by applying the red dots to the lip of the platter.

8 Allow all the paint to dry completely. Bake in the oven at 150°C/300°F/ gas mark 2 for fifteen minutes (or follow the manufacturer's instructions if different), or apply a spray varnish.

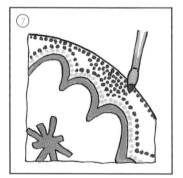

OLIVE grove

ARTIST: Maureen Galvani

colors

The Mediterranean theme and colors of the pasta bowl and oil bottle are perfect for a supper on a warm summer evening. The design is so simple, you'll want to paint a whole dinner service!

You will need:

A bisque pasta dish and oil bottle
Masking tape
A pair of compasses and a pencil
Tracing paper
Under-glaze paints including purple, mustard yellow, and green
A palette
Fine and medium brush
Water, for washing your tools
Glaze

1) Wash your bisque pasta dish and oil bottle with clean water. Allow the bisque to dry.

2) To decorate the pasta bowl, stick a small piece of masking tape onto the center of the bowl. Put the point of your compasses in the middle of the masking tape and draw circles around the center of the bowl.

3) Using tracing paper and a pencil, trace the olive leaf design (on page 60) around the edges of the bowl using the technique described on page 10. Remove the masking tape and trace the olive design in the center of the bowl.

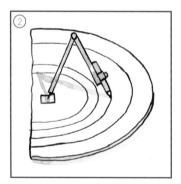

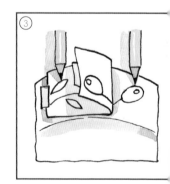

44

4) Shake your paint pots well and pour your color onto your palette. Paint each colored band in turn using a medium brush—remember to rinse it each time you change color. Allow the bands to dry and then paint a second coat of each color.

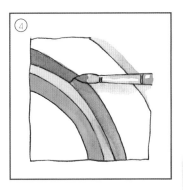

5) Use a finer brush to paint the olives and the leaves. Paint the olives on the bowl's lip last to avoid smudging your design.

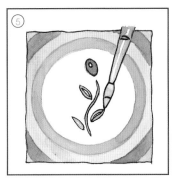

6) To decorate the oil bottle, stick small pieces of masking tape around the body of the bottle to create a straight line around the middle.

7 Use your medium brush to paint stripes of color starting at the top of the line and moving your brush down to the base. Apply two coats of each color, allow to dry then remove the masking tape. Use the same colors to paint the stopper of the bottle.

8 Trace the olive leaf design on either side of the bottle and just under the spout then use your fine brush to paint them.

9 Apply two coats of brush-on glaze and leave the bisque to dry overnight. The pasta bowl and oil bottle can then be placed in a kiln and fired at a temperature recommended by the glaze manufacturer.

HANDY HINT:

As well as using masking tape around the middle of the oil bottle you could also use tape to ensure the vertical stripes are straight and crisp.

WEDDING wishes

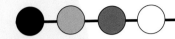

ARTIST: Hannah Berridge

colors

A wedding plate is a wonderful gift for a bride and groom, who will appreciate its unique, hand-crafted nature. The center design can be inspired by the couple's wedding invitation, theme, color, or chosen flower.

1. Clean your plate with soapy water to remove any dirt or grease. Shake your pots of paint well before beginning to paint.

2. Plan your design by sketching the plate on paper first. To get the spacing of the letters and date correct, draw a line down the center of the plate. Count the number of letters in the names and the date—don't forget the ampersand symbol. Work out which letters are in the middle, write the second half of the letters first, and then write the first half of the letters, working back from the center.

You will need:

A glazed plate
Black, white, purple, and green
    ceramic paints
A pencil and paper
Card and scissors
A marker pen
Masking tape
A pair of compasses or small plate
A sponge
A palette
A fine brush and a medium brush
Water, for washing your tools
Spray varnish (optional)

48

3 Cut a horseshoe template out of card, making it symmetrical by folding the card in half and cutting it when folded, or you could use the template on page 62.

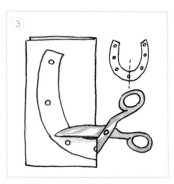

4 Now draw your design onto your glazed plate with the marker pen. Draw round your horseshoe template twice, overlapping the motif in the middle of the plate.

5 Place a small piece of masking tape in the center of the plate. Use the compasses with the marker pen, putting the sharp part of the compass on the tape. Alternatively, you could draw round a small plate. This will be your guideline for writing the names of the bride and groom and the date of the wedding in marker pen. If you make a mistake, use a damp sponge to wipe the marker away.

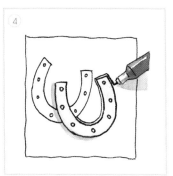

6 Shake the paints well and pour them onto your palette. Using a fine brush, paint the outline of the horseshoes and ribbon in black. Allow the paint to dry for one hour.

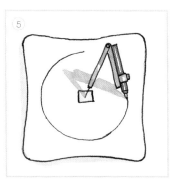

7 Using a medium brush, paint the names and dates. For a funky look, make the end of each stroke thicker by pressing slightly so the bristles splay out at the end of the letter. Allow the paint to dry for one hour.

8 Mix the black and white paint together to make a mid-gray then use a medium brush to fill in the center of the horseshoes.

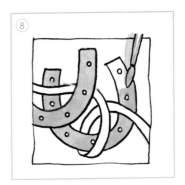

9 Then wash the brush well and paint the ribbon using the purple. Allow it to dry for one hour.

10 Use the marker pen or a pencil to put small lines and dots where you want the roses.

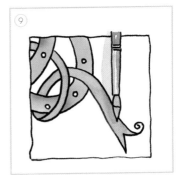

11 Use a fine paint brush to create the roses. Start with the fine, purple spiral. With green paint, add the long stem and leaf.

12 Allow the paint to dry completely. Bake in the oven at 150°C/300°F/gas mark 2 for fifteen minutes (or follow the manufacturer's instructions if different), or apply a spray varnish.

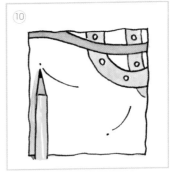

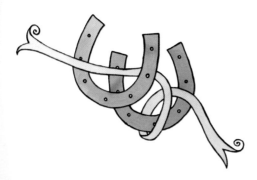

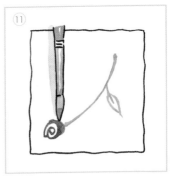

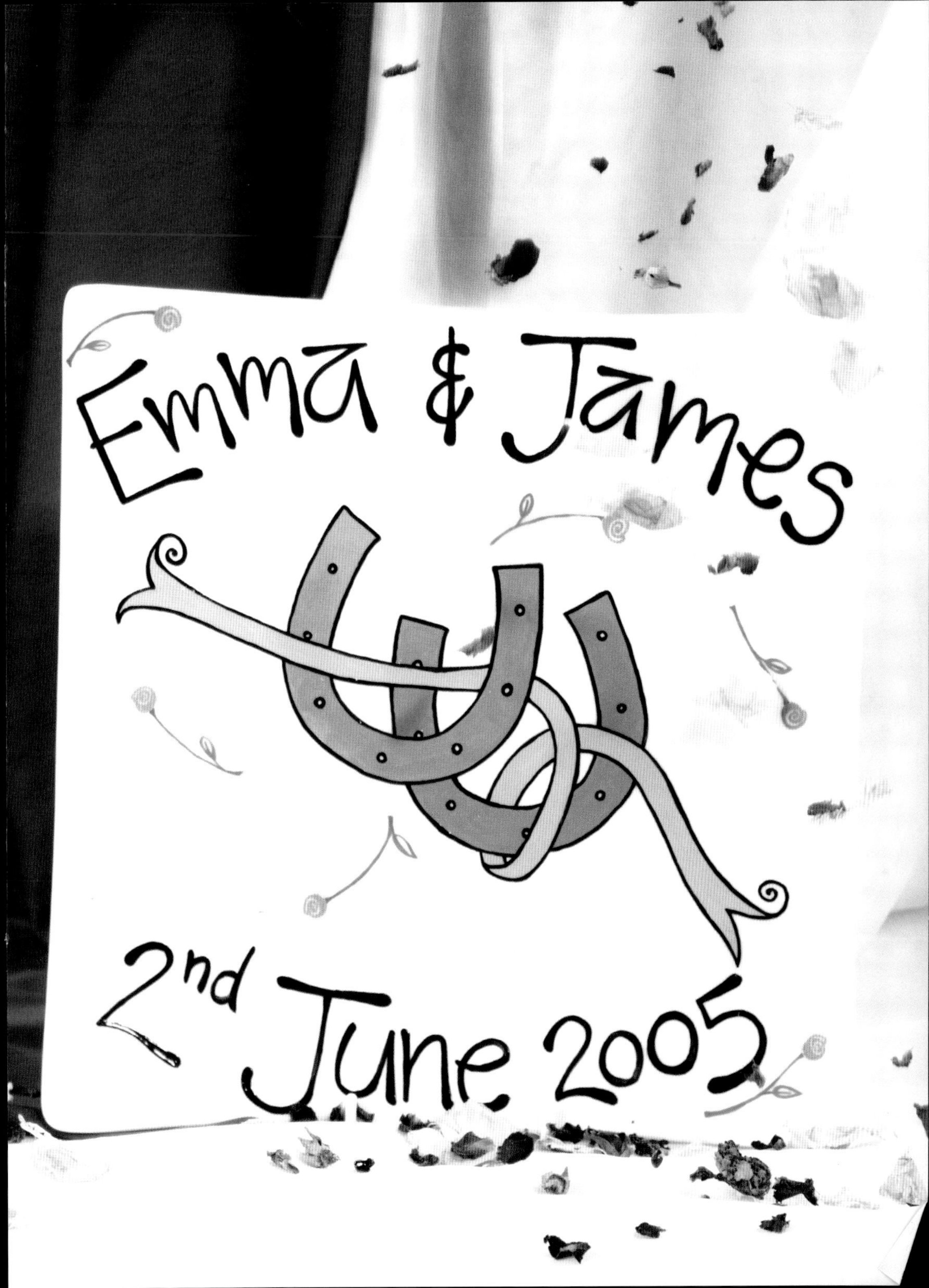
Emma & James
2nd June 2005

FIRST steps

colors

This stunning plate has been created to celebrate the christening of twin boys and is a superb example of how a ceramic can capture an occasion. Using techniques such as stamping with the babies' feet and pencil work by the guests at the christening, this one-off masterpiece will be treasured for many years. There are three stages to making the plate: the footprints, the christening messages, then the completion of the decoration.

1. Wash your bisque serving bowl with clean water. Shake your pots of paint well before beginning to paint.

2. Clean the baby's feet and find a friendly volunteer to help you. An extra pair of hands is very useful to help with the footprints.

3. Shake the paints well and squeeze a generous amount of paint onto your palette. Use your sponge to dab paint onto the baby's foot. Make sure you cover the entire surface.

ARTIST: Esther Macgregor

You will need:

A large round bisque serving bowl

Under glaze paints including black green, blue, yellow, and red

A palette or paper plate for your pair

A sponge

Water, for washing your tools

A pencil and paper

An eraser

Masking tape

A compass

A fine brush and a medium brush

Tracing paper

Paper towels

Glaze

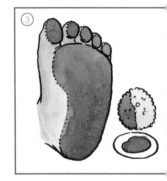

4) The best results are achieved by pressing the plate onto the child's foot rather than standing the baby on the plate. Do one foot at a time, and don't forget to do both feet. It may take several attempts to get prints you are happy with; simply wash your sponge in clean water and wipe away unwanted prints. Wait for the plate to dry then try again.

5) Plan the center name(s) and dates on a piece of paper, drawing a line in the center of the plate. Count the number of letters and numbers and write the second half first. Write the first half of the name and date, working back from the center. Place a small piece of masking tape in the center of the plate. Place the tip of the compasses on the masking tape. With the pencil, draw a circle around the outside of the footprints. This will be your guideline for the names and dates. Remove the masking tape.

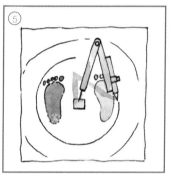

6) At the christening, the godparents of the twins have each written a message for the babies. Ask each godparent to write their message in pencil. They should write clearly and not press too hard. Other guests may like to write a note as well.

7) Use your pencil to mark the top and bottom of the circle. You can now write the names and dates on your plate, referring to the plan you made on paper.

8) Pour some black paint onto your palette. Using a medium brush, paint over the center names and dates. Use a fine brush to paint over the messages and signatures of the guests.

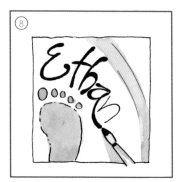

9) Allow the paint to dry and then repeat. The second coat of paint will ensure that the black paint has been applied evenly. Remember that all the pencil marks will disappear when the plate is fired in the kiln so don't worry if there are smudges or mistakes on the plate.

10) Now trace some designs of vehicles (see page 63 for templates) and transfer them onto the plate randomly, to add color in between the signatures.

11) Paint the blocks of color to the vehicles, or your chosen motifs. Allow the paint to dry and add a second coat of each color.

12) Use your fine brush to outline the vehicles and add detail in black paint, allowing the paint to dry before adding a second coat.

13) Apply two coats of brush-on glaze and leave the plate to dry overnight. The plate can then be placed in a kiln and fired at a temperature recommended by the glaze manufacturer.

To our darling boys,
You have already brought us
so much happiness, always look
after yourselves & each other, &
whenever you need me, I will be there
All my love
Auntie Caroline
x

Dear Freddie,
Reach out,
Live your dreams
And ride fast bikes!
Geoff

Freddie!
Learn to face the
sun & shadows
will always fall
behind you
All my love,
Rachel x

Always stay young
at heart and
have fun!
love KerryAnne xxx

So proud to be your
Godmother, I will
always be there for you too!
Big kisses Mallory xxx

Freddie & Ethan
29th May
2003
Christened

Ethan,
Always be happy,
healthy and have
a smile
Love Alastair

Live life to the full
but most of all
be happy!
with love
from Lorraine
x

May all the love
& luck in the
world be yours.
Love Always
Louise
x

TEMPLATES

TREE OF LIFE
pages 18-20

SAFE SAVINGS
pages 26-27

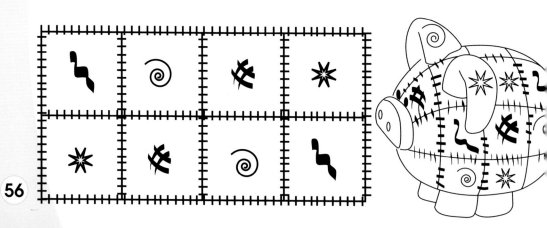

abcdefghijKlmn opqrstuvwxyz

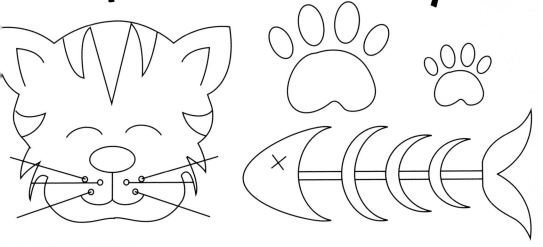

Baa baa black sheep

CITRUS FLAVORS
pages 35-37

TIME FOR TEA
pages 38-40

TEAPOT
LID DESIGN

ABCDEFG
HIJKLMNO
PQRSTUVWXYZ

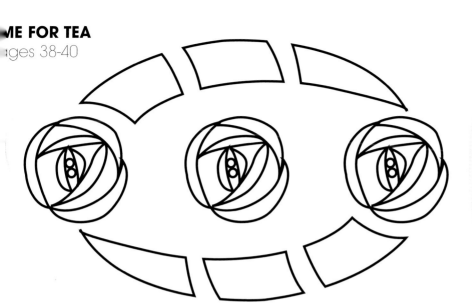

APOT
ODY DESIGNS

SPOT TO DOT

OLIVE GROVE

WEDDING WISHES

pages 48-51

ABCDEFGHI
JKLMNOP
QRSTUV &
WXYZ
abcdefghijklmn
opqrstuvwxyz
0123456789

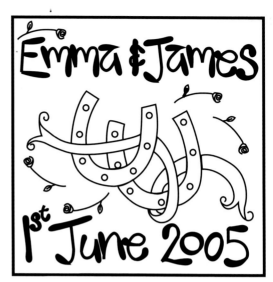

EXAMPLE DESIGN

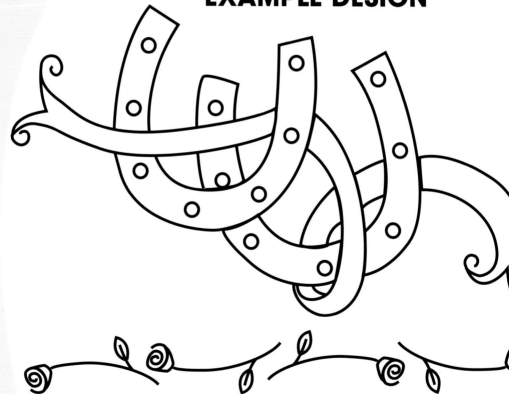

WHAT next?

This book has introduced you to some simple and inspiring ways to decorate ceramics. The projects have used a variety of techniques, often in combination and have given you the opportunity to achieve beautiful results.

In your future projects, you can use the same techniques to create your own designs. Inspiration can come from many places—other pottery, pictures, photographs, and nature. Materials such as leaves, wood, and paper produce interesting prints, as do hands, feet, and even paws.

You can begin to create ceramics for your own use or as gifts for others. With your new-found skills as a ceramics decorator, you will have many opportunities to practice and develop the techniques that you have now learned.